BUILD YOUR BEAUTY BRAND

FIND Your Niche, **CAPTIVATE** Your Clients, And **GROW** The Salon Business Of Your **DREAMS**

HOLLY I. HALL

Build Your Beauty Brand

First Edition

©2015 Holly I. Hall

Illustrations, cover design, art direction and interior design ©Holly I. Hall

All rights reserved. No part of this publication may be reproduced, distributed, or transmitted in any form or by any means, including photocopying, recording, or other electronic or mechanical methods, without the prior written permission of the publisher, except in the case of brief quotations embodied in reviews and certain other non-commercial uses permitted by copyright law.

While all attempts have been made to verify the information provided in this publication, neither the author nor the publisher assumes any responsibility for errors, omissions, or contrary interpretations of the subject matter herein. The views expressed are those of the author alone, and should not be taken as expert instruction or commands. The reader is responsible for his or her own actions. Adherence to all applicable laws and regulations, including international, federal, state, and local, governing professional licensing, business practices, advertising, and all other aspects of doing business in the US, Canada, or any other jurisdiction is the sole responsibility of the purchaser or reader. Neither the author nor the publisher assumes any responsibility or liability whatsoever on the behalf of the purchaser or reader of these materials. Any perceived slight of any individual or organization is purely unintentional.

Quantity sales. Special discounts are available on quantity purchases by corporations, associations, and others. For details, contact the author at www.thebeautysaloon.net.

Printed in the United States of America by CreateSpace
First Printing, 2016

ISBN-13: 978-1523601479
ISBN-10: 1523601477

Dedicated to all hairstylists and beauty professionals who work tirelessly to help their clients see the beauty within themselves

CONTENTS

NEW
glowing with vibrant

Jergens®
ALL-PURPOSE
FACE CREAM
6 OZ.
NET WT.

1

Should You Build A BRAND?

"Your brand is the single most important investment you can make in your business."
—Steve Forbes

Running a salon or working as a booth renter in the 21st Century poses a unique set of challenges for hair stylists and other beauty professionals. Long gone are the days when clients were loyal to the *beauty operator* down the street for their weekly shampoo and set. Clients today are choosy and often hop from stylist to stylist. Internet and social media marketing, as well as the rise of D.I.Y. beauty treatments, courtesy of Pinterest, have presented modern clients with more choices than ever before. As a salon owner or independent stylist, you're sweating bullets.

Maybe you find yourself running more frequent promotions, scrambling to attract new clients and cover your expenses every month. Perhaps you're struggling with how to stand out in an area that has more competing salons than your bathroom has stray bobby pins. You've thrown all the money you can afford at advertising, but it hasn't made much of an impact on your bottom line, and you wish there was a way to make your business more unique and memorable in a crowded marketplace. Or maybe you're in the planning stages of opening your own salon or striking out as a booth renter, and you want to set yourself up for success right from the start.

If this is you, you're not alone. Thousands of salons fail every year. In fact, up to 80 percent of all new small businesses fail within 18 months of opening, and hair salons are near the top of that list. Only a select few salon owners and booth renters are successful and profitable. There are many reasons that salons fizzle and flop, including lack of management experience, low cash reserves, and just plain poor planning.

But, assuming you've planned well and armed yourself with the financing and business skills you'll need, there is one thing you can do that will all but guarantee your success as a salon business owner. What if I told you that no matter where you are in your beauty career, there was a way to set yourself apart and take your business to the top? To make yourself and your salon so unforgettable that clients won't go to anyone else? That just by telling your unique story effectively and consistently, you could attract and keep the exact clients you want, and not only survive, but flourish in this beauty business? Of course you'd want to know what I'm talking about.

The big secret? Crafting a one-of-a-kind, clearly defined brand.

No, I don't mean creating your own line of shampoos. I mean knowing beyond a shadow of a doubt what story your salon is telling and who you're telling that story to. It's as simple as that.

How do I know this? Years before I went to cosmetology school and earned my license, I worked as a salesperson for a major professional beauty supplier. Besides speaking with hundreds of salon owners and stylists in the store each week, I also visited nearly every salon in town on my outside sales route. From small to large, booth renters to huge commission salons, I knew them all. I learned who was struggling to make ends meet, and who was booked solid and growing their income from month to month.

I saw a few salon owners who were thriving, but I saw many more that were one or two slow months away from closing their doors. I quickly recognized that those who were successful had one thing in common—they knew who they were, what story they were telling, and who they were telling it to. Everything that they did reinforced that narrative.

In the years since then, I've worked as a booth renter in a salon, and I've built my own art business selling my work both online and in person at craft fairs. Over the course of the last decade, I have studied what makes successful brands memorable, and have put into practice in my own business the steps I'm going to teach you in this book. Using the same method I will share with you in the following chapters, I have helped other small business owners define their own brands more clearly, never losing sight of my passion for the beauty industry. Hair stylists and beauty professionals, like you, hold a special place in my heart, and more than anything, I want to help you succeed so you can live the life you've always wanted.

In *Build Your Beauty Brand* I'm going to walk you through everything you need to know to design and develop a solid brand to forever anchor yourself in the minds of your clients, and I promise to do it plain English. You'll learn exactly what branding is, what it will do for your business, and how you can start working towards the salon or booth rental business of your wildest dreams right away. I'll take you step by step through creating your unique brand from scratch, and give you the tools to begin crafting your personal brand story. These are the same steps that major brands and corporations use when branding their companies, but with this book, you won't need a sugar daddy with a million dollar budget or a team of advertising executives to get there. I'll demystify the process and break it down into easy to understand language.

"But wait!" You're saying. "I don't have a business degree! I don't know the first thing about branding or marketing. I just do kickass hair (or makeup, or nails, or brows)." I hear you. I know that this can seem a little intimidating at first, but I'm here to tell you that it's easier than you imagine, and the payoff for your business is so huge, when you see what branding can do for your salon, you'll wish you'd started yesterday.

When you follow the simple steps I've laid out in the following chapters, you'll have a new direction for your salon, and a treasure map to success that will simplify almost every decision you'll make for your business going forward. A crystal clear brand identity will serve as the North Star that will guide you as you navigate the sometimes stormy seas of the beauty industry.

When you follow the steps for building a strong brand that I've laid out in this book, you'll:

- Attract more clients

- Retain existing clients

- Stand out in a crowded market

- Grow your business and your income

- Make your salon and yourself unforgettable

Until now, you've been winging it, making decisions for your business defensively instead of proactively. You feel like you're treading water in the middle of the ocean, just barely staying afloat from day to day. At the rate you're going, where will you be a month from now? A year from now? Ten years from now?

If you wait or do nothing, years from now you'll be lucky to be in the same old place in your career, making the same old income. If you're unlucky, you'll have gone under water and out of business. But, if you put the pedal to the metal today and begin writing your brand's singular story, you could be well on your way to doubling or even tripling your income and having the salon business you've always dreamed of.

Don't wait another minute to begin achieving your big, backcombed dreams. Start reading this book today, so that tomorrow you can reap the rewards that building your own fabulous beauty brand will bring. If you're ready to take the first step toward creating the business you've always imagined, head to the next chapter where I'll break down exactly what branding is and isn't, and why it's so important for your salon business.

NOTES

OF PARIS

1504

Marcel
OF PARIS

Lustrapon HIGHLY
CONCENTRATED
SHAMPOO-BASE

2

Branding **101**

"A brand is a story always being told." —*Scott Bedbury*

Let's begin with a short explanation of what we mean when we talk about *branding*, because sometimes businessy jargon and buzzwords can all run together and make a subject seem far more complicated than it actually is. Simply put, your brand is what makes you memorable. It's the images, feelings, words and emotions that come to mind when someone hears your name. As Jeff Bezos, the founder of Amazon says, "Your brand is what people say about you when you're not in the room."

Besides branding, another word you hear thrown around a lot in the business world is *marketing*. The two terms are often intertwined, and therefore confused. So, what's the difference between the two? Marketing is the act of promoting your business through advertising campaigns, social media, and live events.

To illustrate the difference, I'm going to ask you to use your imagination for a minute and picture yourself, not as a hair stylist, but as a baker. Imagine that instead of a salon or beauty business, you own a busy bakery where you make delicious, distinctively decorated wedding cakes. Think of *marketing* as standing in the street in front of your bakery giving away sample cupcakes, talking about your beautiful, tasty confections, fillings, and icing flavors, and offering potential customers a free wedding cake consultation.

Now think of *branding* as the gorgeous, three tiered wedding cake covered in delicate, handmade sugar flowers that sits in the front window, beckoning to brides-to-be on the street. Picture the matching aprons that you and your bakery employees wear which are the same shade of violet that is used on your website, business cards, bakery sign, and brochures. Imagine your logo that cleverly turns the letter *O* in your bakery's name into an image of two linked wedding rings. Taste your signature Lavender Vanilla Bean filling that wedding guests rave about. Can you picture it?

Just like a baker combines flour, sugar, eggs, and butter to make a cake, each and every element of your business and your interaction with the public are the ingredients you will use to build your brand. Like a good vanilla extract distills that heavenly vanilla bean flavor to concentrated perfection, your brand is the pure essence of your business. It's everything you stand for and represent, and defining that essence should come before you do any marketing at all.

WHY YOU MUST DEFINE YOUR BRAND

So now that we've talked about what branding is, let's talk about why it's so important to you as a salon owner. A strong, well-defined brand identity will increase your client base, cement your clients' loyalty, increase your income, and open up new opportunities for your business. Crafting a recognizable brand shows your clients that you have put extra effort and hard work into the image you project to the public. It demonstrates to your clients that you are creative—a *huge* plus in the beauty industry.

Not only does well-crafted branding set your business apart from the crowd, when done correctly, your branding is constantly building awareness of your salon. Even when you aren't actively running ad campaigns or marketing yourself, the foundation you've laid for your brand is working for you and speaking on your behalf.

Another benefit to gutsy small business owners, like you, is that thoughtful, careful branding lets clients know that you are to be taken seriously. It gives the appearance of quality, experience, and reliability that many people only associate with larger, more established companies. Your business will command respect, giving you confidence and enabling you to charge what you're worth. In addition, strong branding puts you at the front of your clients' and potential clients' minds. When they think of your particular beauty specialty, whatever that is, you want them to think of you.

RICHES IN THE NICHES

Speaking of specialties, what's yours? What services are you especially amazing at doing? Are you the best colorist in town? A brow expert? Do you skillfully recreate vintage styles? Maybe you get a thrill during wedding and prom season when you pencil in those special occasion styles on your books. You might be the very best at everything you do, nailing cuts, color, and styling every time, but I'm here to break it to you, doll—you cannot be all things to all people and get ahead very fast.

One of the number one mistakes I see stylists and beauty professionals make is that they try to cater to everyone. Yes, it's true that you should be well versed and knowledgeable about a variety of styles and techniques. You should know how to nail basic cuts and be comfortable with color theory and the science of haircolor. It's important to be well-rounded, but in order to brand yourself and attract the loyal clients you want and deserve, you need to decide what you will specialize in and what you want to be known for.

For branding purposes, you should narrow down your focus to better appeal to a certain type of client. This doesn't necessarily mean that you can't offer a full menu of beauty services, or that you shouldn't strive to improve in every aspect of your career, but you want to define the thing that you're best at, the point where your skill and passion meet in a big, romantic Hollywood kiss. Find the thing that gets your creative juices flowing and makes you come alive, so that when people think of elegant bridal styles or vivid rainbow-colored locks or detailed men's cuts, your name is at the top of their list.

There's a phrase that entrepreneurs often use that says, "The riches are in the niches". This means that when you narrow your focus, or "niche down" to offer services to a very specific subset of customers, you'll have more luck attracting business, and you'll rise to the top of your field more quickly.

When you tell people that you are *the* vintage hair expert in your city, and you have the skills and retro flair to back up that claim, people will believe you. Through specializing in one area and emphasizing your expertise, you will soon become known as a leader in your chosen niche. Not only will you attract more vintage-loving gals and guys as clients, opportunities that you might never have expected will be presented to you. When the local paper does a story on the resurgence of pinup style and a reporter needs a quote from someone who is involved in the scene, guess who will be at the top of her list of contacts. When a period film is being shot in your city and the call goes out for local cosmetologists who can do vintage styles, you'll be in your element.

Branding yourself as a specialist instead of a generalist is the difference between yelling from the top of a mountain, hoping your voice reaches someone, *anyone* who will listen, and addressing a small room full of people who have come specifically to hear what you have to say. When you know who you need to speak to, it will be infinitely easier to speak directly to those people. Stick with me, because in the next chapter, I'm going to help you begin to write your story, and find the people who are waiting to hear it.

MODEL

GRIP-TUTH
HAIRTAINER
SECURITY FOR *EVERY* HAIRSTYLE

APRIL, 1963

IN TWO SECTIONS · SECTION ONE

3

PROFESSIONAL COSMETOLOGIST

The Skilled Hand
of Beauty
RAYETTE
SELECTED
SALON

Wisp-Whirl Coif

Finding Your
NORTH STAR

"A brand is not a product or a promise or a feeling. It's the sum of all the experiences you have with a company." —Amir Kassaei

Are you ready to get down to the nitty gritty of branding your salon? I hope you answered yes, because in this chapter, I'm going to put you through a series of three exercises that will get your gears turning and throw your creativity into overdrive. By the time we're done, you'll know exactly who your target customer is, what your brand position in the market should be, and you'll hold in your pretty, skilled hands all the features and facets of your dream brand.

EXERCISE NUMBER 1: YOUR TARGET CLIENT

Every time you get dressed for work, greet a client, answer the phone, give a shampoo, or hand out a business card, you are telling the world a story about yourself and your salon business. You can put a lot of effort into writing it, but if you don't understand who needs to hear your story, it won't matter how great you are at telling it.

So, who are *you* talking to? What type of person is your dream client? Defining your target customer is a fundamental aspect in this entire process. Just like the base of that tiered wedding cake we imagined, knowing your audience is the foundation on which you begin to build your unique brand, so don't skip this step! I'm going to walk you through an easy exercise that will help you define exactly whose business you are trying to attract.

For this exercise, you'll need a piece of paper. You can open a word processing document if you'd like, but I'd recommend starting a small notebook (or the digital equivalent) just for keeping your thoughts and notes about your branding all together in one place. It doesn't matter how you get the information down, just that you actually record your answers somewhere that you can refer back to them again and again.

I want you to think about your ideal client, the person you envision serving in your dream salon. Perhaps you already have a real life favorite client and you want more just like her. Maybe you have yet to open your salon or booth rental business and have no regular clients of your own. That's okay too. This doesn't have to be a real person. You're going to invent her or him right now. I want you to get very, very specific here.

Keeping in mind the niche you're focusing on and the income levels in the neighborhood and city where you're located, you want to define this person's:

- name

- gender

- age

- occupation and job description

- hobbies

- relationship status

- any and all other personal details that come to your mind

Go into every tiny, miniscule detail. It might feel strange and unnatural to you to do this. That's okay. Do it anyway.

When I say to define your target customer's name, I mean I really want you to name this person. Mentally walk through how he or she spends their day at work. Name the restaurants, stores and clubs they frequent. Do they have children? A spouse or partner? How do they spend their free time? What kind of music do they listen to? What car do they drive? Do they have any pets? What is their favorite band? Color? Food?

Got it all written down? Great! Now I want you to find a photo online or in a magazine to represent this target customer, assuming he or she isn't someone you know in real life. If you do know them, but you aren't close, don't ask for a photo of them "for a project", unless of course your plan for making your brand unforgettable involves being creepy as hell. Hey, no judgement here. I'm all for letting your freak flag fly.

There are two ways to do this next part. You can either get crafty with a poster board, a glue stick, and a stack of magazines, or you can do as I've done and create a secret board on Pinterest dedicated to your target customer. Besides his or her photo, pin things to this board that your target customer loves. Using the list you made, pin (or glue) photos of clothes, rooms, makeup, books, quotes, baby animal memes, food—anything that you imagine he or she adores. Try to see the world through their eyes. You can really have a lot of fun with this. It's like trying on a new identity. Here, I'd like to emphasize the importance of flipping the privacy toggle to *secret* for this Pinterest board, especially if your target client is a real person. Failing to do this will put off some serious creeper vibes, and that's not good for business.

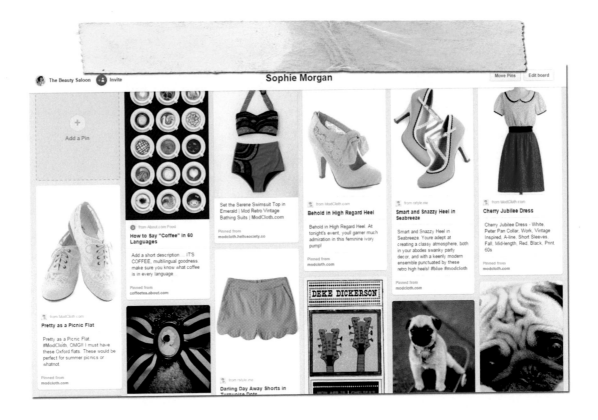

This exercise may seem silly or unnecessary, but by doing this, you are getting yourself inside the minds of the people you are trying to reach. This benefits your brand and your future marketing strategy. However strange this feels, sit down and spend some time on it because I can guarantee that you're going to come away with a clearer picture of where to steer your brand.

EXERCISE NUMBER 2: YOUR BRAND POSITIONING

In addition to defining the customer you're speaking to, it's crucial to decide your brand's position in the local market and how it differs from your competition. To do this effectively, you'll need to identify and communicate what makes your business unique, and what it is that you offer to your clients that the salon down the street doesn't. Ultimately, your positioning will determine where and how you advertise, what type of clients you attract, and even what you can charge for your services.

To understand what we mean when we talk about brand positioning, you first need to discern what makes your salon different from the rest. For some businesses, this means being the first of its kind, the fastest, or perhaps the least expensive. For others, it may be exclusivity or luxury. You'll need to decide whether to market your brand as high-end or entry level, premium or inexpensive.

There are three core concepts that determine a brand's positioning.

1. **Functional** positions solve a problem or provide a benefit to customers. Examples are: fastest, cheapest, good value, one stop shopping, or highly specialized service.

2. **Symbolic** positions enhance a customer's self-image, inflate their ego, or give them a sense of belonging within a group or society. Examples are: luxurious, exclusive, fashionable, or famous.

3. **Experiential** positions provide a treat for the senses or offer a one-of-a-kind experience, Examples are: relaxing, immersive, or a unique destination.

While it is certainly possible that your brand might offer a little of each of these concepts to potential clients, just as we narrowed down a specific niche of your beauty talents to spotlight, selecting only the most relevant and outstanding concept will help you craft your brand's story. Your brand positioning is vital to growing a prosperous business because you can't be effective in your marketing and promotional efforts if you don't know what you provide for the clients you serve. Yes, you provide haircuts or color or waxing or nails, but what you're really selling to your clients is an idea, sometimes referred to as a *brand promise*. You're selling them time by offering fast, walk-in service. You're selling them improved self-image with your superior knowledge of the latest haircolor trends. You're selling them indulgence with your signature rose petal pedicure. Again, this is where so many salon owners make the business-suffocating mistake of trying to be all things to all clients in a mad scramble to get business wherever, and from whomever, they can. You cannot define your target client as a wealthy, childless young executive, and then run back to school haircut specials in September. Get it together!

If you've identified the niche you'll be focusing on, positioning your brand will almost always flow naturally from there. For example, if your niche is romantic bridal updos, and your target client is Brittany the young, professional, bride-to-be, you already know that you'll be charging a premium price for special occasion styling. Because weddings are such a significant event, clients expect to pay more for styling services on their special day, especially with a stylist who is known for being the Local Bridal Hair Goddess. While other stylists in your area run discounted styling specials during wedding season, hoping to attract new business, the sophisticated updos that you've become known for will be sought out by discriminating clients, positioning your hairstyling business as an upscale brand. Because of this, and because Brittany is tech savvy and has lots of disposable income to spend on her dream wedding, you won't advertise in the local newspaper or offer discounts to reach her. Instead, you'll buy a few, targeted online ads and set up a branded, sophisticated booth at the local wedding show. Taking the time to think through your brand positioning will assist you in making smarter decisions for your business, and it will help you reach your target clients more easily.

I think it's important to mention that if you want to charge premium prices and position your brand as a luxurious indulgence, you'll need the skill, attention to detail, and high-end service to back up your claim. As my mama always says, "Don't let your mouth write checks that your butt can't cash."

EXERCISE NUMBER 3: NORTH STAR LIST

Now that we know *exactly* who we're talking to, the really fun part of writing your brand's story begins. For this exercise, I'm going to ask you to use good old-fashioned paper and pen. I truly feel that creativity and thoughts flow more swiftly and freely when you're writing by hand. This method is a quick and easy way to begin defining your beauty business or salon brand, and it all begins with a list.

Because this is such a vital part of the process of developing your brand identity, don't attempt this exercise when you can't give it your undivided attention or you feel rushed. Wait for a quiet time when you are relaxed and in a spot free of distractions. You might even want to sit down with a beer, a warm beverage, or an entire box of wine. Spend a few minutes picturing your dream salon in your mind. Imagine walking through the front doors, past the reception area and the shampoo bowls, all the way to your station. Notice the sights, sounds, and smells around you. Once you've conjured up a vivid mental picture, pick up your pen and begin to write.

I want you to make a list of the first words that come to mind when you think about your ideal business. Don't analyze your thoughts or aim for perfection as you brainstorm. This should be a free and messy stream of consciousness writing exercise. Just list any and all of the words or phrases that appeal to you. List objects, emotions, feelings, colors, eras, movies, books, music, and even scents that evoke the feel that you want your salon or booth rental business to have. Keep writing until you can't think of anything else. Fill your paper if you can. There are no wrong answers. The idea is just to let all of the contents of your brain spill out onto the paper in a beautiful mess.

After you have emptied your brain of all these descriptive words, take a good look at your list. You will probably begin to see an overall pattern emerging. Strike anything that doesn't seem to mesh with the overall feel of the list. The words that remain will form what I call your *North Star List*, because it will guide you as you navigate every future decision you'll make as a beauty business owner. Congratulations! You're well on your way to creating an original, outstanding brand identity that's one hundred percent you. We'll talk more about how to use this list in the upcoming chapters.

4

A REVOLUTIONARY NEW CONCEPT IN HAIR ROLLERS

$1.50 PER DOZ.

RUBBA ROLLA

1. Faster and easier to use.
2. Hair dries quicker.
3. Soft and comfortable.
4. Economical — no end paper needed.
5. Simple to wash and sterilize.
6. Gentle to tinted, bleached, and fragile hair.

ASK YOUR DEALER SALESMAN

1 PLACE WET OR DRY HAIR ON THE ROLLER

2 FLIP END FLAP OVER HAIR

3 PULL UP ON HAIR

4 ROLL TOWARDS SCALP USE PICK OR CLIP

GORHAM ASSOCIATES INC. 230 Boylston St., Boston 16, Mass.

Smooth Little Puff

Choosing A **NAME** For Your Salon

"They say a name expresses the thing it stands for, but I wonder if it isn't the other way around—the thing gets more and more like its name." —Haruki Murakami

It's hard to overstate the importance of selecting the right name for your salon. Your business's name makes the very first impression on potential clients. We've all seen (or worked in) some unfortunately named salons. If you've not yet opened your salon or freelance beauty business, you're starting with a clean slate, so it's worth it to think very carefully about the image you want to project with the name you choose.

There are many options when it comes to naming a business. Like naming a child, it is an individual choice, but there are some guidelines that will help you choose a name that you and your employees will be proud of, and one that will stand the test of time. In this chapter, I've included some prompts to jump start your brainstorming and get those naming gears turning. I'll also address some advantages and disadvantages to each type of salon name.

GETTING PERSONAL

If you're striking out on your own as a mobile freelancer or booth renter, or even opening your own salon, you have the option of naming the business after yourself.

Choosing to use your own name can be a smart move if you want to advance your personal beauty career while keeping your options open for the future.

One advantage to using your own name for your beauty business is that you will have total control over your own image. *You* are your brand. Exceptional or exceptionally awful, people will associate their experience at your salon with you. Clients will also have an easier time finding you or following you from a previous place of employment. Another bonus is that your talents and beauty know-how will follow you through your entire career. All of your advancements and notoriety—both amazing and appalling—will be tied to you personally, not to a salon name.

There are multiple advantages to using your own name, but there are also a few things to think about before you name your salon or beauty business after yourself. Before you take this route, ask yourself the following questions.

Is your name scalable? By that, I mean can it work for a second location if your salon grows and expands? If your sights are set on eventually building a large regional or national salon chain, do you want to attach your family's name to such a business? And if you do ingrain yourself into the fabric of a flourishing company and later decide to sell, will you lose the rights to use your own name in future business ventures? It has happened before. No one has a crystal ball, of course, but it's worth examining all the possible outcomes when you are using the name your mama gave you.

Is your name unique? No offense to the Jane and John Smiths of the world, but if you have a very common name, not only will it be hard for your business to stand out from the crowd, you could run into trademark issues down the road.

Is your name hard to pronounce? If you have one of those names that people are constantly asking you to spell, or one that people have trouble pronouncing, you might be setting yourself up for headaches. Many clients would rather avoid your business altogether than risk embarrassment by trying to pronounce a word or name they don't understand. Don't believe me? Have you ever gone into a fancy coffee shop or restaurant and been so overwhelmed and intimidated by menu options you couldn't pronounce that you just blurted out, "I'll take a black coffee, please"? No? So, that's just me then?

LOCATION, LOCATION, LOCATION

If you're ready to put down roots—ahem, *new growth*—in the location of your dreams, naming your salon after the neighborhood can be a smart branding move. Especially if your city is having a cultural renaissance, you can capitalize on local pride, honor the location's history, and embed your business into the community by choosing a location-dependent name for your salon.

If the street or building where your salon will be located is notable, naming your shop after the address can guarantee a permanent place in the minds of your clients. *Salon Ten O Six* and *42 Broadway Ave.* are two examples of this type of name.

The neighborhood may offer inspiration when thinking of a name. For example, in Oklahoma City, the neighborhood that once housed the Film Exchange District, where theater owners came to screen and lease films for their movie houses, is now known as Film Row. If you were opening a salon there, you could take this to its literal conclusion and call it *Film Row Salon*, or you could choose something more subtle and figurative, such as *Old Hollywood Hair* or *Silver Screen Beauty Shop*.

In addition to your city and neighborhood, don't forget your state or county's particular assets and quirks when dreaming up names for your salon. State emblems such as birds and flowers can offer unusual name inspiration for your business. Choosing a name that relates to your locale can be an excellent way to brand yourself and make your salon memorable, just be certain that you plan to be in that location for the foreseeable future.

HISTORICAL INSPIRATION

As in the Film Row example above, history can be a wonderful source of inspiration, especially if you specialize in vintage styles. If you love a particular era, admire a specific historical figure, or you are located near where a notable historical event took place, it may provide the spark that leads to the perfect name.

Besides local history, beauty and hairstyling history can offer business names that brand you or your salon with a vintage vibe. For example, several modern salons specializing in vintage hair and makeup have successfully used plays on the words "pin up" and "pin curl" to get their retro aesthetic across. Try leafing through your cosmetology text books or vintage women's magazines for beauty-themed name inspiration. Certain terms will evoke specific eras, which can work in your favor if you want to project a vintage image.

Finally, don't overlook personal and family history when in search of a name for your beauty business. Using a beloved grandmother's name or the name of one of your personal sheroes or heroes can be a meaningful and unique approach. This type of name will give you a wonderful springboard when creating a brand story because it's so personal for you.

OTHER SOURCES OF NAME INSPIRATION

Pop culture is another rich source of inspiration. You can use the following as jumping-off points when thinking of name ideas.

- Movie titles
- Song titles
- Song lyrics
- Book titles

- Poetry and literary quotes

As you go about daily life, take notice of everything around you and stay open to inspiration, because it can come from the most unlikely places.

A BRAND EXPERIENCE

One of the easiest options for naming a beauty salon, and the one most full of possibility, is to choose a name that reflects the brand experience you wish to provide. Here is where the North Star List you made in chapter 3 comes in handy. Take a look at the words that you wrote down. Do any of them stand out? Maybe the name of your salon is right there in black and white! More likely though, a pattern or a general feeling has emerged that you can translate into the perfect salon name.

The best brand names are suggestive and evoke images in the minds of customers. The name you choose should suggest something about the spirit or personality of your brand. A great name is also open-ended and unrestrictive. *Candy's Cuts* is cute, but it might be hard to market your skin care services with a business name that implies that you only offer haircuts.

As I brainstormed for my fictional salon brand, a pattern of feminine glamour and refinement emerged. I wrote things like *roses, crystal, mirrors, pink, pampering,* and *luxury,* which led me to write *powder room.* That antiquated phrase evokes the sense of femininity, sophistication, and vintage beauty rituals that I want my brand to convey. *The Powder Room* has just the right mix of charm and style, and it is flexible enough that I could take my branding in quite a few directions. Of course, your list of words and the feelings you wish to evoke with your name and your brand will be different from mine, but your personal list should offer the same sort of guidance when choosing a name for your salon or freelance business.

An excellent way to gather more fuel for your name brainstorming fire is to put each of the words from your North Star List into an online thesaurus, such as

Thesaurus.com. When I entered the word *rose* from my list, I got the words *red, blush, flush, pink, rosette,* and *rouge.* While not part of my original brand brainstorming, *rouge* is a retro makeup term that definitely has potential as part of a vintage-inspired salon name, or could perhaps be used for a future product or service. The idea is to go down the rabbit hole, following each word or phrase that speaks to you, using a combination of the thesaurus, Google, Pinterest, and even YouTube to make connections and spark ideas. Write everything down to refer back to later. This is how truly unique business names are born.

When naming your salon, don't forget about your target market and your ideal customer. What will appeal to them? It's important for you to be happy with your name, but if it doesn't attract the clients you want, it doesn't matter how much you love it. Select a name that evokes the feelings you want your clients to have about your business. Do you want them to associate your salon with luxury? Cutting edge, fashion-forward styles? Relaxation? Keep that concept at the forefront of your mind when selecting a name.

You should also plan for all the ways that clients will encounter your salon name out there in the world, whether in print, television ads, or in conversation. Select a name that looks good on paper and rolls nicely off the tongue.

As you ponder potential names, think all the way through the branding concepts each one suggests. What style, color schemes, era, and decor does each name hint at? When deciding between a few possible candidates, always select the name that offers the most possibilities for unique branding touches. For example, instead of going with *Candy's Cuts,* which would be limiting since Candy hopes to offer skincare and makeup services in her salon, in addition to haircuts, *Candy's Beauty Bar* would be a better choice. The name is open-ended enough to encompass numerous beauty services as her business grows and expands, and the candy theme suggests an array of clever branding opportunities. From bright or pastel candy colors on the walls, to business cards featuring candy bars or peppermint stripes, the possibilities for Candy to reinforce her branding are endless.

TOP THREE SALON NAMING MISTAKES

There are three giant, enormous, colossal mistakes that I see repeated time and again when it comes to salon names. At best, these types of names are unoriginal. At worst, they are unprofessional. Avoid these common naming mistakes at all costs.

1. **Clichés**. Don't choose a name that is overused in the salon world. *A Cut Above* might be clever, but it returns hundreds of results on Google, four in my state alone.

2. **Weird spellings**. Don't use alternate or difficult spellings or punctuation in your business name. If you're forever spelling and explaining your salon's name, you're making a bad impression on clients. If you have to say that yes, you know *Krazy Kuts* would normally be spelled with C's, but your salon's name is spelled with K's, you're making an unprofessional first impression. As Alexandra Watkins says in her book, *Hello: My Name Is Awesome*, having to repeatedly explain your business's name is like apologizing for your brand, and who wants to start out a business relationship with an apology?

3. **Awful puns**. Don't ever, for the love of Vidal Sassoon, use a pun as a salon name. Why do so many salons do this? While you may think that a punny salon name will cause clients to squeal with delight over your cleverness, in reality, most of them are rolling their eyes and groaning at your dad jokes. This is not the way you want potential customers to encounter your business for the first time. Even if they take a chance on you and love your work, do you think clients will be thrilled to recommend Tammy at *Hair-2-e-Tan-ity* to all their friends and family? We've all seen these dated and cringe-worthy sorts of salon names: *The Grateful Head, Hair Force One, Shear Madness, Combing Attractions, The Mane Event, Cuttin' Up*. And then there are the

names that combine a pun with intentional misspellings such as *Jus Teezn*. Those names make me need to lie down. Forever. In a grave. Why would you choose to make the name of your business a joke, especially one that could be offensive? *Finger Bang*? *Nail Me Good*? *Snip Tease*? Okay, now you have blown way past unprofessional straight to *bless your heart* territory.

WORKING WITH AN EXISTING SALON NAME

Maybe you've picked up this book because your existing salon business could use some polishing. You already have a business name, and the recognition and clientele you've built depend on sticking with what you've got. If your business is really stagnant and you've outgrown your name, don't be afraid to make bold, new choices and completely rebrand. Don't worry about existing clients finding you. In this age of Google and social media, no one will have trouble tracking you down, and future clients will never know you as anything but your new identity. You can even reroute an old web address to your brand new site if necessary. However, if it's really not an option to start from scratch, don't get your weave in a tangle. While not ideal, there are ways to mold an existing business name into a brand you love.

To quote L.M. Montgomery in her book *Anne of Avonlea*, "That's a lovely idea...Living so that you beautify your name, even if it wasn't beautiful to begin with...making it stand in people's thoughts for something so lovely and pleasant that they never think of it by itself." You have the power to beautify your brand so thoroughly that you will be able to influence the associations and images that come to your client's minds when they think of your salon name, even if it's not the one you'd choose today. As you write your wonderful new brand story, your salon's name will just be part of the overall client experience. It will come to mean exactly what you tell people it does. No one ever would have associated computers and technology with apples before Steve Jobs came along. Now, when we hear the word *apple*, right up there with the sweet, crunchy fruit that doctors fear, MacBooks and iPhones come to mind.

NEXT STEPS

Now that we've gone over how to find inspiration for your business's name, let's talk about what you should do once you've narrowed your choices down to a few possible candidates. Even if you've settled on the perfect name, there are a few things you should research before you place an order for new business cards.

First, you'll need to find out if anyone else is using the name you've chosen. Google is your friend here. If you find that someone else is using a salon name you have your heart set on, it's not necessarily a deal breaker, but remember that the goal is to stand out from the crowd. Stay away from names that are overused, especially in your local area.

If you live in the U. S., you'll next want to search The United States Patent and Trademark Office's website to see if anyone has trademarked the name you want to use. This may seem unnecessary for a small, local business, but you never know how big you might grow or where you'll want to take your brand in the future. Trademark infringement could cost you lots of legal fees and headaches down the road, so don't get too attached to a name until you've ruled out existing trademarks.

Next, it's time to shop for a domain name. This is so critical. It's the 21st Century, and your business *must* have a web presence. If the exact domain is not available, don't get your knickers in a wad. Try adding a modifier, such as "salon", "beauty", or the name of your city. With few exceptions, you should avoid hyphens and numerals, and never choose strange or alternate spellings. You want something memorable, simple to say, and easy to understand. Don't be afraid to think outside the box when it comes to selecting a domain name.

Going back to my fictional salon, The Powder Room, let's imagine that thepowderroom.com is already taken or is out of my budget. I could certainly add "salon" to the end or buy the .net version–and I will–but since I can have multiple domains routed to one website, why stop there? Your website's URL offers an often overlooked branding opportunity. I could also purchase *meetmeinthepowderroom.com* or even *powdermynose.com*. Either would be catchy and unexpected in an advertisement or splashed across the back of a T shirt.

Small, quirky touches like these ensure that your brand won't be forgotten. Now that you have some ideas and guidelines for choosing a name, it's time to take action toward building your beauty brand. In the next chapter, I'll show you how to think through every aspect of your visual branding to make yourself memorable to every client that sits in your chair.

STYLING

4

5

COMB-OUT

6

MODERN BEAUTY

POSNER'S
Wig-Klean

CLEANS AND RES̶̶ WIGS
WIGS AND HAIR 136

SHRINKING or MATTING

Fringe 'n Flares

5

BEAUTY SHOPPE

Your **VISUAL** Brand Language

"Design is the silent ambassador of your brand." —Paul Rand

In an industry so focused on looks and outwardly visible beauty, you must define a strong visual brand language for your salon or independent beauty business. Taking great care to present your business thoughtfully will position you not only as a serious businessperson, but as an expert on beauty. If you don't put thought into the way you present the visual aspects of your business, make no mistake—clients will notice. Given the choice between a salon with a strong visual brand and one without, all other things being equal, clients will gravitate toward the business that presents a cohesive brand image.

So, what do we mean when we talk about your salon's visual brand language? We're simply talking about the colors, shapes, fonts, and design styles associated with your business. It's that straightforward. It just means putting thought into making your salon's logo, signage, decor, business cards, and online presence look cohesive and connected.

If I asked you what mental images came to mind when I said *Target*, I'd bet that pretty close to the top of the list would be a red bullseye. It's on the store's sign, featured in their commercials, on their website, and on their social media pages. It's even repeated in a pattern on their shopping bags.

In addition to their ubiquitous logo, you will notice a similar look to all of the video and print ads that Target puts out. The same sorts of images, bright with color and modern simplicity, dominate everything the company shares, and we all know that if you need help from a Target employee, you need only look for the nearest person in a red shirt and khakis. Target, like all large corporations, has spent hundreds of thousands of dollars carefully shaping their visual branding. Studying the branding of larger companies is a wonderful way to get new ideas and learn what works. You can then put your own spin on these concepts, and apply them to your own business's branding strategy.

As you begin planning your salon's visual brand language, you'll want to have your North Star List handy. Remember that this tool is your compass for navigating all of your branding decisions. The words, images, and feelings you want to be associated with your brand are going to give you a framework for building your brand's visual identity.

YOUR LOGO

Let's start with your logo. A logo is a graphic representation of your brand. Coming in a close second after your business's name, your logo is one of the first impressions potential clients have of your brand, so it needs to be well-designed and look professional. The main function of a logo is customer recognition. Just as you immediately think of Apple Inc. when you see that image of a bitten apple, a great logo is memorable and instantly recognizable.

There are three main types of logo design:

- **Iconic/Symbolic**: A single icon or image. Two examples of this type are the aforementioned Apple and the Nike swoosh.

- **Logotype/Wordmark**: Your business's name in a stylized font. Think Coca-Cola or Google.

- **Combination Mark**: A graphic with both text and an icon. Starbucks has one, as well as Twitter.

A logo is critical for your business, but there are a few ways to go about getting one, depending on your budget.

HIRING A DESIGNER

Of course, the number one way to get the perfect logo for your business is to hire a graphic designer. These professionals are trained to distill the essence of your brand down to a single, refined graphic image that can work to represent your business across a variety of applications. While it will be money very well spent, hiring a design firm is the most costly option, and far out of the reach of most small business startups.

A more affordable option, if you do have some coinage to spend, is an online design service such as 99designs.com. You have a couple of choices with this service.

At the time of this writing, for 99 U. S. greenbacks, you can choose from an array of ready-made logos that will be personalized for you. For example, a search for "beauty salon" returns hundreds of results. But, don't search only for the obvious, beauty-related logos. Try searching some of the words from your North Star List for unique logo designs. While this won't be a custom designed, one-of-a-kind logo, it can be an affordable way to get a decent logo for your business when you're on a tight budget, if you don't have the design skills to do it yourself. You can always upgrade later!

For a custom designed logo, 99designs.com also gives you the option of running a design contest for your logo design job. With packages starting at $299, you fill out a design brief detailing your wishes for your logo, and dozens of designers compete for the job. Each returns a design, and you pick the winner.

If you'd like the help of a graphic designer to create a logo or other branding materials, but don't have the financial resources to hire one, consider bartering your hair or beauty services in exchange for design work. It never hurts to ask! If you find a designer who agrees to an arrangement such as this, make sure to lay out clear terms with a simple contract stating what the designer will provide to you in exchange for the specific services you will offer in return. Of course, the other alternative for gutsy beauty entrepreneurs is to roll up your sleeves and Design It Yourself.

D.I.Y. LOGO DESIGN

Since you've chosen to build a career in this beautiful beauty industry, chances are, you have an eye for color and design. If you don't have the dough for design help, you can use that artistic eye of yours to tackle the job of designing a logo yourself. You can do this, dollface, and I'm going to show you how.

To begin, find four or five companies whose logos you love. Do you notice any similarities between them? Are you drawn more to logotypes or to wordmarks? Ask yourself what it is about them that speaks to you. Is it their simplicity? Their elegance? Their unexpectedness? The more logos you study and analyze, the easier it will be to replicate their success in your own design.

There are five basic principles to keep in mind when designing an image to represent your business:

1. Think simple. The more concise, the better.

2. Use no more than three colors. We'll talk more about color in the next chapter, but if you're not a pro, too many colors can look amateurish.

3. Use no more than two fonts. It's generally best to use two complimentary letter styles and no more.

4. Your logo must work for a variety of applications. Your logo should read well in color and in black and white, and in both print and digital forms.

5. Add an optional, branded tagline. A few well thought out, catchy words (two to five) after your business's name can reinforce your brand and communicate what you're about, though your logo should be able to stand alone when necessary.

LOGO DESIGN TOOLS

If you work well with pencil and paper, feel free to begin your logo development by sketching out some basic ideas and layouts. Eventually though, you'll want to move to the computer. If you don't have a program like Photoshop or Adobe Illustrator, there are two online tools I recommend for basic, do-it-yourself logo design.

GraphicSprings.com allows you to begin designing your own logo for free using a library of images and fonts. Then, once you're happy with your final design, you pay $39.99 (at the time of this writing) to download the files. This is a great option for absolute beginners because the site is easy to use and offers some simple and straightforward choices to help you create a basic logo. Avoid the over complicated image choices. Simplicity is the name of the game.

The Powder Room

Here is a mock-up logo I created using GraphicSprings for my fictional salon, The Powder Room, to show you what's possible with this tool. Keeping in mind the feel of my North Star List, I wanted something that read as vintage and feminine. Font choices are limited on GraphicSprings, but a typeface called *Limelight* had a 1930's feel that fits with the brand identity I'm establishing. I chose an image that was reminiscent of both a powder puff and a dancer's feather fan, appropriate considering that *burlesque* was one of the words on my North Star List.

If you're a little more confident in your design skills and want something totally free, Canva.com is one of my most favorite online tools. It's free to use, and there are a variety of fonts, shapes, and icons you can combine to create your own logo, as well as thousands more graphic elements that cost just one dollar each. Referring again to my North Star List, I made a few mock-ups using this tool to illustrate what is possible. You'll also notice that I've used the tagline "vintage salon" to further reinforce my branding.

The Powder Room
vintage salon

A WORD ABOUT FONTS

When choosing the fonts you'll use to create your logo, it's important to think about the image you're trying to project. Once again, refer to your North Star List. It might sound strange since we're just talking about letters on a page or screen, but different typefaces communicate different feelings. All fonts have a personality and a purpose. Fonts can read as masculine or feminine, modern or vintage, and playful or serious. In the above example, I chose a sophisticated, feminine font with an antique feel called *Great Vibes* to communicate the glamorous, vintage vibe I want for my salon.

When combining fonts in any design, you'll want to choose two that contrast nicely. Don't use two different cursive fonts together, for example. If you use a bold, all-caps font, contrast with something lowercase, thinner, or more flowing. There are no hard and fast rules here. You have to play around until it looks balanced. You're looking for that sweet spot where peanut butter meets chocolate and it just *feels right*.

ALL CAPS
with cursive

Cursive
+
sans serif

Fancy Script!

SUBTITLE OR TAGLINE SMALLER AND IN ALL CAPS

SMALLER HEADING

BOLD

Play Around
UNTIL IT FEELS RIGHT

AND SMALL TAGLINE

Besides the font or fonts you will use to create your logo, you'll want to select no more than three additional fonts that you will consistently use when designing digital or printed items for your business. A clean, bold typeface, an easy to read cursive font, and a basic sans serif font will give you a variety of options and combinations for everything from Facebook and Instagram graphics to salon service menus and business cards. By using the same few fonts everywhere that your business is represented, you will subtly reinforce your individual brand without creating visual clutter and chaos.

WORST FONT MISTAKES

Spend very much time studying fonts and you will begin to recognize specific typefaces as you encounter them in the big, wide world. Spend very much time studying graphic designers, and you will begin to recognize which poorly designed, outdated fonts drive them batty and inspire them to compose frothy-mouthed internet rants. Design snobbery aside, there are some fonts whose use will communicate a very undesirable message about your salon business. These five dated, threadbare fonts belong in a trash can in the year 1999. Avoid them at all costs.

1. **Curlz**. Overused, especially in the salon world—Get it? It's called Curlz? Like hair curls? LOL!—this 1995 font just won't die.

2. **Comic Sans**. A favorite of out-of-order toilet sign makers the world over, this childlike font was originally created for use in comic book style speech bubbles. Never, ever use this font for anything, unless you have a salon that caters to children with a comic book theme—which could actually be really cool now that I think about it. However, there are still better font choices.

3. **Papyrus**. Like Ancient Egypt meets the 80s. Walk like an Egyptian far, far away from this font.

4. **Jokerman**. Do you want your salon brand to resemble the menu from a 1990's Tex-Mex restaurant owned by a killer clown? No. The answer is *no you don't*.

5. **Bleeding Cowboys**. This 2007 grungy, Western font is newer than the rest, but has already become overworked and exhausted. It makes eyes bleed on everything from bro country album covers to the logo of your cousin's kitchen-based tattoo business. Cowgirl up and choose a better font.

While I can't give you an entire graphic design course in this chapter, the tips and guidelines I've shared should get you started on the right foot. My advice is to open a design program or one of the online resources I've mentioned and spend a day playing and creating until you land on a design you love. For further study when it comes to logo design, font selection, and other graphic design projects for your business, I recommend the excellent book, Graphic Design for Non-Designers by Tony Sedden and Jane Waterhouse. In the next chapter, we'll continue defining your visual brand language through the use of color.

NOTES

FIS-6881

6

Fashioned with Fullness

Branding Your Salon With COLOR

"I found I could say things with color and shapes that I couldn't say any other way— things I had no words for." —Georgia O'Keeffe

Color is one of the most essential tools in your branding toolbox. It is is the visual component people remember most about a brand, followed closely by shapes and symbols, then numbers, and lastly, words. Color can evoke emotion, convey a message, and make your business utterly unforgettable. Because the right colors can communicate so much about your business to potential customers, it is impossible to overstate the importance of color to your overall branding plan.

When you read the name Coca-Cola, what color instantly comes to mind? Red, naturally. It's the same with Starbucks' green, and Home Depot's familiar orange. Color is so vital to a company's branding, that in a few special cases, large corporations have been able to trademark specific shades for use in their industries, such as Cadbury purple and Tiffany blue. Mega brands such as these have all used a signature color to cement their brand image in our minds. That should be your goal as well when selecting colors to represent your salon. Your aim should be to employ a signature color so completely that it becomes a trademark inextricably linked with your brand, like Johnny Cash's pitch black wardrobe, Barbie's hot pink everything, or the way that particular shade of robin's egg blue is synonymous with Tiffany &

Co. In this chapter, I'll give you some guidelines and tools for selecting the perfect color scheme to represent your salon business.

THE PSYCHOLOGY OF COLOR

The subject of color and how it affects our emotions and buying habits is a complex one. Colors and their associated feelings and emotions can be subjective and vary widely based on personal history and cultural norms. For example, while in much of the Western world white is associated with innocence or cleanliness, in Chinese culture it's the traditional color of funerals and mourning. Colors may also read differently depending on how they are utilized. Black, when used a certain way, can be upscale and sophisticated, but it's also traditionally the most rock and roll of all the colors. Black is both uptown and downtown, elegant and badass, depending on context.

It would be impossible for me to explore the nuances of each color in this chapter—that's a book unto itself. Besides, you likely have your own feelings and opinions about each color of the rainbow. In general though, here are some connotations of each color of the spectrum.

Red: exciting, bold, aggressive, active, confident, powerful

Orange: extroverted, spontaneous, warm, exotic, fun

Yellow: energizing, optimistic, cheerful, happy, creative

Green: soothing, natural, healthy, growth, prosperity, clarity

Blue: peaceful, calm, spiritual, credible, open, intelligent

Purple: creative, majestic, original, stimulating, royal

Pink: youthful, romantic, feminine, love, playful

Brown: earthy, natural, masculine, traditional, woodsy

Black: modern, sophisticated, deep, fashion-forward, magical, edgy

White: pure, soft, noble, clean, airy, clinical

Gray: classic, understated, timeless, trustworthy

According to a study about the effects of colors on products and branding, the most effective use of color was how appropriate it seemed for the brand's positioning in the market. So what does this mean? In the simplest terms, the colors you choose to represent your salon should fit the image you want to project. That's straightforward enough, isn't it?

To break it down even further for our specific purposes, if you own a day spa that specializes in relaxing facials, massages and pedicures, soothing greens or earthy, neutral colors make more sense than energizing yellows and oranges. A barber shop catering exclusively to men would be better served by using colors that read as more masculine, such as red, black, or blue, rather than pastel shades. It sounds like common sense, but you'd be surprised at how many businesses just slap colors around haphazardly.

COLOR THEORY

As a beauty professional, you're probably more attuned to color than many, but as a refresher, let's talk about some basic color rules and define some terms.

Primary colors: Red, blue, and yellow. All colors are created from these three.

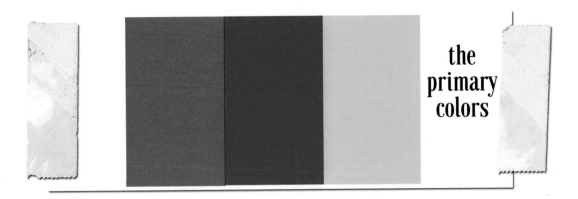

the primary colors

Hue: The purest form of a color. A color that has no black or white added to it.

Shade: A hue mixed with black.

Tone: A hue mixed with gray.

Tint: A hue mixed with white.

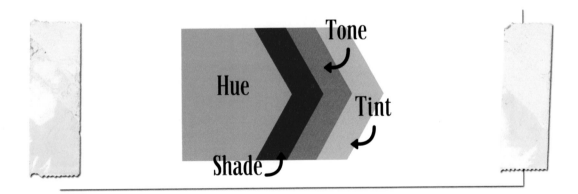

Tone

Hue

Tint

Shade

Complementary colors: Colors that cancel one another out when combined. You can find the complementary color for any hue by looking directly across the color wheel from it. When mixed, they create a neutral color, and when paired, they make each other "pop".

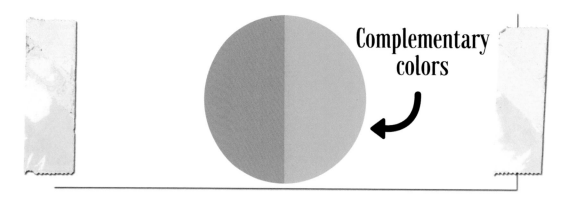

Complementary colors

Analogous colors: Colors next to each other on the color wheel.

An Analogous color scheme

Monochromatic colors: All the tints, tones, and shades of a single hue.

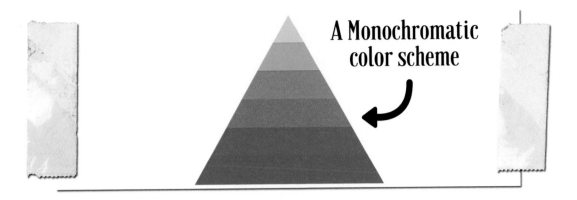

A Monochromatic color scheme

Brightness/Value: How dark or light a color is.

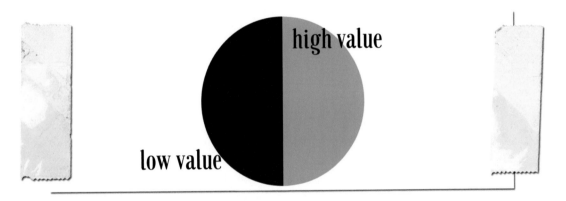

high value

low value

Saturation: How rich or vivid a color is. Hot pink is very saturated, while pastel pink is less so.

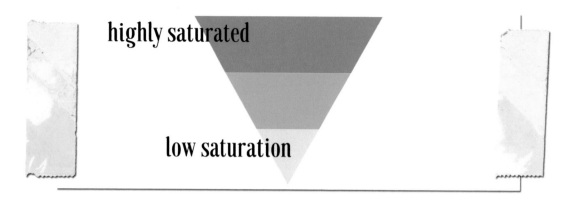

highly saturated

low saturation

It's useful to also understand some color terms associated with digital and print applications, such as:

Hex code: Short for "hexadecimal code", a series of 6 letters and numbers after a hashtag that computers use to name specific colors. A hex code looks like this: #c3d476.

RGB: Stands for "red, green, blue". In this color model, red, green, and blue light are added together in various amounts to reproduce millions of colors. Used primarily to represent colors on electronic devices.

CMYK: stands for "cyan, magenta, yellow, and key black" and is a type of printing process that uses ink in these four colors to create hundreds of colors.

SOURCES OF COLOR INSPIRATION

You might wonder, with so many possibilities, how do you decide on the perfect colors for your business? The first step is to think about the image you want your salon to project. For help with that, you'll need your North Star List. Am I starting to sound like a broken record? I told you that list was important!

Did you happen to write down the names of any colors on your list? If so, you may already know exactly which shades will speak to your ideal client. Besides your

North Star List, refer to the Pinterest board you made for your ideal customer. What colors did you pin to your board? Remember that your ultimate objective is to appeal to your target client, so go with what you think will resonate with her.

If after creating your list, defining your ideal customer, and naming your salon you're still struggling with finding the perfect color scheme to define your brand, never fear! There are so many sources of color inspiration. Here are some ideas to get you started.

- Your favorite outfit can be a great starting point. Do you own a dress you just love? One that makes you feel like a million bucks every time you put it on, just the way you want your clients to feel when they leave your salon? Chances are good that the colors you feel dazzling in are going to brand your business as so very you. While we always want to appeal to our target client, part of building a long lasting brand is authenticity, so never be afraid to be true to yourself.

- Photographs are one of my very favorite places to begin searching for color scheme inspiration. Look for a photo that evokes the emotions you want your clients to have when they think of your salon business. Whether it's a soothing forest, an energizing street scene, or even a nightmarish hellscape like the one below, you can use an online resource like Colrd.com's Image DNA tool to break it down into a color scheme you can use.

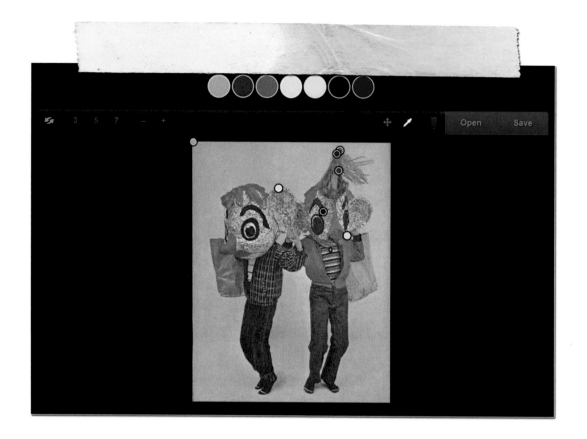

- Vintage paper ephemera such as old magazines, books, postcards and greeting cards can be an excellent source of color inspiration, especially if you want to brand your business as vintage. Going for a 50's look for your salon decor and business materials? Where better to look for color schemes than in printed material from the era you are trying to evoke.

- A work of art that speaks to you can provide a color scheme that may be perfect for your business. Just as interior designers often take color inspiration for a room from a painting or framed print, you can translate your favorite artist's use of color into a branding scheme.

- Spend some time browsing the wallpaper sample books at your local home improvement center. The artists who create these patterns have already done the work of combining colors in pleasing ways. As a bonus, you can use touches of the inspirational wallpaper to decorate your salon.

- Another type of art that is often overlooked is the cover art of your favorite albums. Look through your record collection (or your iTunes playlist) for color combinations that speak to you.

CREATING A DYNAMIC SCHEME WITH THE CUPCAKE RULE

When deciding on a color scheme to represent your business, unless you're a pro graphic designer, it's best to use no more than three core colors. Begin by choosing one leading color, and then one or two accent colors. You can expand your palette by using different shades and tints of these two or three core colors. When all of the values in a scheme are equally intense, the colors compete for your eyes' attention and can appear overwhelming and harsh. By using a mix of light and dark color values, you'll create a livelier, more dynamic color palette. For example, if you like the way red and green complement one another but want to avoid a clashing, overly Christmasy palette, you could go with a scheme of mint green, creamy white, and red. While those would be your three central colors, you could also sprinkle in some pink touches (a tint of red) or a deeper green here and there for spice.

Once you've narrowed down your choices to the three main colors you'll use for your visual branding palette, you'll want to avoid using all three shades equally in any given application. To achieve a professional look, it helps to think of your color ratio as a cupcake. Your main color and the bulk of your scheme is the cake, your first accent color is the frosting, and your third color is the cherry on top, the little touch that makes the other colors pop. Sweet and easy.

The Cupcake Color Rule

"Pop" Color - - - - - - - - - ->

Accent Color - - - - - - - - ->

Main Color - - - - - - - - ->

FAVORITE COLOR TOOLS

Here are some of my favorite online color tools to help you as you craft the perfect branding color scheme for your beauty business.

- Colourlovers.com is a creative community where users create and share color palettes and patterns, and discuss color trends. It's an endless source of color inspiration.

- Design-seeds.com offers fresh and beautiful color scheme eye candy, and features the ability to search for pleasing palettes containing a specific shade.

- Colrd.com lets you look through thousands of users' color schemes based on photos, and create your own with the image DNA tool.

- Imagecolorpicker.com is an extremely useful tool for finding the hex color codes from a photo or web page.

- Coolors.co is a very cool site that generates random color schemes that you can alter and refine until you find true love.

For a list of links to all of these online tools and more, download the free Quick Start Branding Action Plan at www.thebeautysaloon.net/beautybrandfreegift.

PAINT YOUR BRAND EVERYWHERE

So now you've learned how to effectively use color to brand your beauty business and firmly fasten yourself in your clients' minds. You've been inspired and chosen the perfect colors to represent your salon, but maybe you're wondering where and how to use these colors. The answer? Everywhere. Use them everywhere—your logo, your website, your Facebook page, your signage, your business cards, your smock or apron, and your decor. Anywhere there's an opportunity to use color, use your branding color scheme. Make your chosen colors so integral to your salon business that your clients find you popping into their heads whenever and wherever they encounter your signature scheme in the world. And now that you've chosen your perfect colors, the next chapter is all about how to bolster your brand through your salon's decor, without breaking the bank.

PINK OR
BLUE
VISORS

Crowned
the

SPEED
KING

with

"MERCOTH____
MAGIC'

The LAST WORD in Dryers! Bre___
record for sales! SPEED KING h___
thing you want in a Dryer!

CENTU__Y LINE
DE LUXE ___AIRS

Ultra-modern design . . . u___atable for
VALUE and EYE-APPEAL! 13__ors.

See Your Speed King De___

de Graff

PRODUCTS COMPANY

Boost Your Brand
With Your DECOR

"Style is a way of saying who you are without having to speak." —Rachel Zoe

Have you ever been to a restaurant where the interior looked like Richard Simmons' closet, and your mom's Pinterest account drank 4 Loko together until they threw up? Or worse, one where no effort to decorate was made at all, and the fluorescent lighting and beige walls look like something from the set of *Orange Is The New Black*? Sometimes the service or food in these places is awesome enough for you to return, in spite of the shabby surroundings, but they probably won't be at the top of the list when you're looking for a spot to take a date or an out-of-town guest.

Believe it or not, as a former salesperson for a major professional beauty product distributor, I've visited many salons that fit the descriptions above. Just as in the restaurant business, atmosphere and attention to detail matter when you want to impress a guest and secure their continued business. In an industry so focused on looks and visual appeal, why in the name of Mr. Teasie Weasie don't more salon owners try to get their decor right?

I have said it before and I'll say it again, ladies and gentlemen, your branding should be at the forefront of your mind in every decision you make regarding your salon or beauty business. Remember your North Star List? Tape it somewhere you can refer back to it again and again. Refine and edit it over time if you need to, but always keep in mind the vision you have for the brand you're building.

When you're ready to pick out a paint color, choose wallpaper, buy reception area seating, build or buy stations, or choose mirrors and art for the walls, make sure that your choices fit with the theme of that list. This doesn't mean you can't go for an eclectic look with your decor, or that you can't shop with a budget—quite the contrary! It simply means that you are laser focused on telling your brand's story, and that you have a clear vision for what your salon's decor says about you and your brand. Just as with all the decisions you've made so far, keep your ideal client in mind when you decorate your salon. Who is he/she? What are his/her tastes? Decorate through their eyes. Pin all of your decorating ideas and inspiration to a Pinterest board, just like the one you made one about your target customer.

THE SALON FURNISHINGS TRAP

It would be ideal if enterprising salon owners could shop for salon equipment such as hydraulic chairs, shampoo bowls, and dryer chairs with the same sort of selection and variety as an interior designer furnishing a living room. Unfortunately, our choices in salon equipment today seem to be limited to black, black, and more black, with very few exceptions. Look, I like black as much as the next girl. It's fairly neutral, reads as modern, and doesn't show stains, but it can be a bit limiting when it comes to designing your salon's interior.

Once upon a time, salon-owning beauty operators had a rainbow of choices when it came time to furnish their shop. Professional trade magazines of the 1950s and 60s contain advertisements for hydraulic styling chairs and dryer chairs in the popular pastel, candy-colored shades of the day. Salon equipment from the Swinging Sixties could often be found in bright colors and floral patterns. While other options besides basic black do exist for today's salon owners, most are quite expensive and often require custom ordering and costly shipping fees. If you've picked up this book, I'm going to assume that you don't have a million dollar decorating budget and a professional interior designer on your payroll. Let's face it—a lot of us are limited to what we can find used on Craigslist, or what's in stock at our local beauty supply chain store.

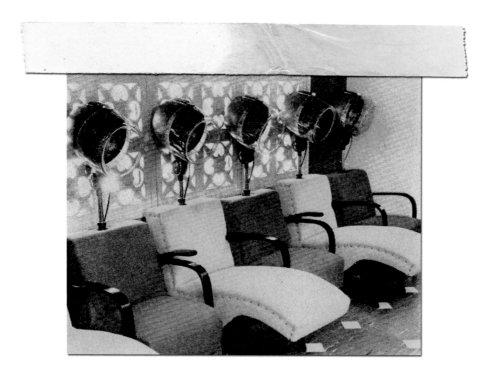

Just because you're working with run-of-the-mill equipment, it doesn't mean that there aren't dozens of opportunities to add serious style to your salon's decor. I believe that many salon owners fall into the trap of thinking that everything they purchase for their salon's interior needs to have been intended for salon use. Yes, it's true that you must have a hydraulic chair, and there's no substitute for a shampoo bowl and reclining chair, but beyond these core pieces of necessary equipment, there are a thousand ways to think outside the salon box when designing your shop's interior.

Your salon's reception desk, waiting area, retail display, and work stations are all prime spots for creativity and details that support your brand story. In these areas, you are limited only by your imagination. There's no rule that says that your styling stations have to be cabinetry purchased from a salon equipment distributor. Essentially, you need a mirror, a surface, and some drawers for tools and products. Vintage vanities, antique dressers and buffets, and even wall-spanning, built-in cabinets from a home improvement store can all be unexpected and unique solutions for your work stations. In fact, nothing is stopping you from taking cabinets out of the equation all together in favor of floor-to-ceiling framed mirrors and a simple rolling cart.

I can't count the number of salons I've visited that had boring, dated commercial reception area seating. Your salon shouldn't greet customers with the same furnishings as the Department of Motor Vehicles or a gynecologist's office. Clients come into your salon to be transformed and pampered—not to feel like they're waiting for a pap smear.

One of the most beautiful salon seating areas I've ever seen consisted of a gorgeous, antique sofa covered in red velvet, a couple of mismatched, comfortable armchairs, a vintage coffee table, and a pair of 1950's lamps on end tables. It was a cool, artistic living room vignette tucked into a corner near the salon's front window. Clients began their salon visit in comfort and creative style, and almost seemed reluctant to leave their cozy reading spot when stylists came to retrieve them at their appointment times.

All sorts of furniture pieces can be repurposed for use in the salon. Estate sale finds, thrift shop scores, and IKEA basics can be stand-ins for retail shelving, color mixing bars, and more. Any chair can become a dryer chair with a rollabout dryer. Often, for the same price you would pay for a piece of commercial salon cabinetry, you could hire a local woodworker to create something to your exact specifications. As a bonus, you'd be supporting a fellow small business owner. You may even be able to barter your beauty services in exchange for carpentry work.

But back to that hydraulic chair—the only rules are that it be in good working order, and that it is covered with a material that sheds hair and is easy to clean and sanitize. Search for previously-loved bargains, and don't be afraid to get creative with a styling or shampoo chair that's a little rough around the edges. If you're confident in your crafty skills, you could try your hand at upholstery with colorful vinyl or retro oilcloth, or use a special paint made especially for vinyl to give it a facelift.

TELL YOUR STORY WITH DECOR

By now you know that all of your decorating decisions should be made with your brand story and target client in mind, but there are a few other details to think about. When decorating your salon, it's important to consider the area where your business is located. Is your salon nestled within a historic neighborhood? It's best to work with the building's character and choose appropriate accents from the period. While you do want to stand out from the crowd, be sure not to go with a theme that is so *out there* for the location that you run the risk of clients just not getting it. A glossy white and chrome interior will probably be off-putting in a small, rural town, no matter how much you might love it, not to mention that your ideal client for this type of salon is nearly nonexistent in your area.

Just as we talked about branding yourself as a specialist in one niche, whether it's vintage, color, or eyebrows, you want your decor to reflect the hair, makeup, or nails that you so expertly produce. If you primarily execute asymmetrical cuts and vivid fantasy colors, your brand, and therefore your salon's decor, should reflect your edgy vibe. The same goes for vintage specialists—your favorite era's colors and decorating style can carry your branding through to your salon's atmosphere.

Remember that you are telling a story about yourself and your business with every decorating detail. Use your branding color palette on everything from accent walls to picture frames, and spend some time thinking through all the ways you might reinforce your branding through interior design. Drawing from the Candy's Beauty Bar example, Candy could incorporate touches of peppermint-striped wallpaper, mirror frames painted with jellybean hues that pop against a chocolate-colored wall, and large glass apothecary jars in her retail area that contain candies in her branding color scheme.

Referring back to my North Star List for my fictional salon, The Powder Room, it's easy to picture an opulent, Old Hollywood interior with dusty pink velvet draperies, curvy furniture, glided mirrors, crystal chandeliers, and cut glass bowls full of fresh roses. Glamorous, antique touches like these would support the image of vintage, feminine luxury that I want my brand to reflect. While your own brand story will be different, it's vital that your salon's decor be thoroughly branded and thoughtfully carried out.

TIPS FOR DECORATING ON A BUDGET

Clever decorating doesn't have to cost and arm and a leg. Thrift store finds and some fresh paint can go a long way toward a beautiful, branded salon. The magic of Pinterest has placed thousands of D.I.Y. decorating ideas at our fingertips, and a bit of elbow grease and creativity are all it takes to transform a space. Here are some cost effective ways to decorate on a dime.

- Repurposing furniture and objects in unexpected ways is not only cost-conscious, it's also smart branding. Try to look at garage sale pieces through fresh eyes. Who says you can't use a vintage refrigerator to store products or tools, or that an old hair dryer bonnet can't become a light fixture?

- Paint or paper one striking accent wall. We've discussed the importance of color when it comes to branding, and paint is an inexpensive way to style your space. Using a bold, unexpected shade or a patterned paper on one wall can elevate the entire salon and distract from ho hum furnishings.

- Go big or go home. Invest in one or two big furniture pieces for storage or retail display. Too many small cabinets and tables scattered about can look cluttered and untidy. A massive, junk store chandelier could become your salon's focal point with a few coats of paint and some new wiring. It's best to spend your money where it will make the most impact.

- Don't forget fabric. Because we're dealing with hair clippings and chemicals, fabric doesn't belong in every corner of your salon, but some heavy floor-to-ceiling curtain panels can soften hard lines and warm up a cold reception or waiting area. Shop for discount drapery fabric, hem the ends, and hang a couple panels in the corners of your front window.

- Make your own art. Paint a large canvas in a single, strong color for a modern, minimalist design scheme. Frame a large section of wallpaper or fabric in a bold pattern with inexpensive molding from the hardware store. Hang a grouping of objects for a distinctive focal point, such as pretty plates, hand mirrors, old scissors, or empty mismatched picture frames all painted the same shade. Almost anything can become art when you think outside the box.

OVERLOOKED SALON AREAS

As you plan your space, don't neglect some commonly overlooked areas. The first thing your clients will see when they visit your salon is your signage and the shop's exterior. Make a favorable first impression with a branded sign and inviting touches like a large planter of flowers or a welcome mat. Peeling paint, pigeon poop, dead leaves, and cigarette butts will leave a bad taste in a client's mouth before she even steps foot inside your salon. Because most small salons rely on walk-in business, it's vital that your outdoor space is attractive and welcoming. Think about what potential clients see as they pass your front window. Seasonal decorations and displays should be kept fresh and rotated frequently.

While your clients will spend the majority of their salon visit in your chair, it's important to remember all the other out-of-the-way spots where they will find themselves. Restrooms, coffee and drink stations, and any other salon areas clients will see should be clean, uncluttered, and stylishly decorated. One spot that it often doesn't occur to salon owners to decorate is the ceiling, especially above the shampoo area. An unexpected color or a patterned wallpaper can be eye-catching here, but it's really only necessary that there are no cobwebs or water stains to detract from an otherwise wonderful appointment in your salon. Paying attention to even the tiniest details is part of branding every aspect of your client's experience—a subject we'll explore in more depth in the next chapter.

Hair Shapers and Blades

EACH OTHER

EDWARD WECK & CO., INC.
DIVISION OF STANDARD INTERNATIONAL CORP.

8

OWI-16623-C

"first with the finest"

dainty puff of glamour
Dream-Puff
New bouffant-size
Andre Fantasies
Sleep Cap. #944 —
$1. retail

wet-weather wonderful!
Rain-Belle
Chiffon/plastic
reversible hood by
Andre Fantasies.
#1305 — $1. retail

Ask your distributor or write for samples:
Please send samples of #944 and #1305.
Dept. M

Branding Your Client's EXPERIENCE

"Making promises and keeping them is a great way to build a brand." —Seth Godin

Up until this point, most of what we've talked about has been focused on attracting new clients to your salon. Yes, it's crucial that you stand out from the competition and draw first time customers, but if a clients' first experience in your chair doesn't live up to her expectations, there's a good chance that she won't be back. If you've successfully presented a compelling and cohesive brand identity, enticing a new client to make an appointment, you've essentially made a promise to the client about what she can expect to gain by trusting you with her hair, nails, or face. Keeping that promise should be your primary focus from the moment she steps foot inside your salon. Smart business owners know that a satisfied client is the best advertisement for your salon and services, and the smallest details really do matter where branding is concerned.

HELLO, GORGEOUS

How many times have you called a business and been met with frustration at how your call was handled? Either the phone rings over and over with no answer, or the line is picked up by a hurried, sometimes rude, receptionist. Or worse, you're abruptly put on hold and sent to dead air for what feels like a year. It's enough to make you spitting mad and to never want to deal with the place again. Take a lesson from these third-rate businesses, and don't let all of your hard work and smart branding be overshadowed by bad phone practices in your salon.

Branding your client's experience should begin from the moment she first speaks with you or a member of your staff, whether in person or over the phone. No matter how busy the salon is, or how harried you or your employees are, answer the phone with a smile. While smiles over the phone may be unseen, they are definitely heard. Answer each phone call with energy and enthusiasm as though you are genuinely happy to hear from the caller on the other end, and there's nothing else you'd rather be doing than speaking with her. Since those callers are the clients—and potential clients—that keep your bread buttered, you *should* be happy to hear from them. A phone call to ask about services or pricing could be someone's very first experience with your salon, or it could be a longtime client calling for the hundredth time. Whatever the case, you are building a relationship with the person on the other end of the line, and it's up to you and your staff to make it a positive one.

Think of each call as an opportunity to gain a new client and present your brand story. An excellent way to do this and to ensure consistency with your salon's phone practices is to adhere to a scripted greeting. I'm not talking about reciting robotic telemarketing sales pitches here, but a short, relevant sentence or two that relates to your branding and your seasonal offerings will be memorable and could lead to increased sales. For example, instead of answering the phone at Candy's salon with a simple, "Candy's Beauty Bar, how may I help you?" the receptionist could immediately begin branding a client's experience with the line, "It's a sweet day at Candy's Beauty Bar, this is Susie. Would you like to treat yourself with one of our Chocolate Peppermint Pedicures?" Right away, the caller knows that Candy's Beauty Bar is unique with a brand identity that is playful and focused on indulgence, and she has been offered a tempting service that she may never have considered otherwise.

Similarly, smart, well-crafted hold and voicemail messages are an overlooked opportunity to reinforce your salon's branding and highlight featured services. A tailored recording describing a signature service or a unique product offering is much preferred to sending clients to scratchy elevator music or dead air. Change these scripts and recordings seasonally to keep them fresh and to reflect holiday offers and promotions.

AMENITIES AND NICETIES

When a client enters your salon, think of her as a guest in your home, and treat her accordingly. As soon as she walks through the door, she should be cheerfully greeted and invited to your chair or a comfortable waiting area, whether by a receptionist or by her stylist. If you are busy with another service, give your client an idea of how long she can expect to wait for you to finish. At all times, salon employees should refer to your guest by her name, and not by the time slot or service for which she's visiting the salon. "Jane is here for you, Susie," is worlds better and more respectful than your receptionist or another stylist referring to Jane as "your 2:30" or, God forbid, "your Brazilian wax".

Just as you would when a guest visits your home, go above and beyond to make clients feel welcome, comfortable, and pampered. Offer a short neck and temple massage with aromatherapy oils, or a small product sample at the end of a service to make her feel cared for and appreciated. Keep a selection of beverages and small snacks available to offer your guests. A hot cup of coffee or tea on a chilly winter day, or a bottle of sparkling water will be appreciated and remembered. Depending on your local liquor laws, you might also offer a glass of wine or a beer.

There is even an opportunity to reinforce your branding here if you choose beverages or treats that relate to your salon's name or brand identity. My upscale vintage salon, The Powder Room, might offer a glass of champagne and a fancy chocolate truffle to guests, reinforcing my brand identity of refined, feminine elegance. A Rockabilly salon or barber shop could offer cold Pabst Blue Ribbon beer in cans, while Candy's Beauty Bar might set up an actual candy bar like those that have become popular at wedding receptions, allowing guests to choose from a selection of small confections bearing Candy's brand colors.

If your brand's story doesn't immediately suggest a signature beverage or snack, channel your inner Martha Stewart and invent one! Create a make-ahead cocktail, either alcoholic or virgin, in your brand's signature color, and name it after your salon, or come up with a name using words from your North Star List. For The Powder Room, I'd concoct a pretty pink drink containing passion-fruit nectar, champagne, and grenadine and call it *Powder Room Punch*. You don't necessarily need to be fancy, just thoughtful.

For most clients, the best thing about a salon visit is the relaxing shampoo. It's the highlight of the service for many people, a chance to unwind and escape the stress of their day for a few moments. So *slow your roll*, and don't make the common mistake of rushing this part of the service. A phenomenal shampoo and scalp massage could gain you a client for life. The same goes for hand and foot massages during manicures and pedicures. A handy trick for bewitching your client when she's at the shampoo bowl is to apply conditioner, and then gently lift and cradle her head in one hand while massaging the back of her neck and the base of her skull with the other hand. The conditioner already on your fingers serves as a massage lotion, and you can wipe off any excess later as you towel dry her hair. This move is scientifically proven to melt clients like butter and cause them to rebook with you—and only you—time and time again. Okay, maybe there's no science behind it, but trust me—it works like a charm. The important thing is to always stay in tune with your client, reading her signals to be sure she is comfortable with what whatever you are doing.

ATMOSPHERE AND AMBIANCE

In any service business, the atmosphere inside the establishment can make or break the customer's experience there. When you choose to take a date to an Italian restaurant with dim lights, private booths, and quiet background music rather than a bright, busy pizza joint, you're basing that decision on the ambiance of the business. Your salon's atmosphere should set clients at ease, and be appropriate for your brand identity. Imagine your salon's environment as the backdrop for a play, where everything the client sees, feels, and hears supports the brand story you're telling. When it comes to branding your client's experience, you are both director and set designer. At least once a week, walk through the front door of your salon and look at everything anew, as if you were looking through the eyes of your target client. When we spend many hours, days and weeks in one space, we can become desensitized to small details that are obvious to others, and, as we've established, when it comes to branding, details are meaningful.

It should go without saying, but every place that your client's eyes will fall should be sparkling clean and free of dust and hair clippings. The front door and windows should be crystal clear with no traces of fingerprints. Your waiting and reception area should be stocked with fresh, up-to-date magazines and hairstyle lookbooks. Discard anything that is tattered or torn. Retail displays should be attractively arranged, fresh, and immaculate, and we've already covered how vital your salon's decor is to your branding.

When designing your salon environment, don't forget about your clients' ears. Music is a neglected branding opportunity in many businesses. Directors and movie makers know that the right piece of background music can take a scene from mediocre to unforgettable, and move viewers to the edges of their seats. The term *mood music* exists for a reason! By playing music that enhances the atmosphere inside your salon and relates to your brand identity, you can affect your clients' perception of your brand, and add to their overall experience. For instance, if you own a salon specializing in vintage styles, your clients should be greeted with melodies that hark back to the era of the hairstyles you create, while a fashion-forward salon might choose current electronica or hip hop.

Carefully curated music is one of the best ways to brand a client's experience, but when it comes to playing music in your salon, a word of warning—there are laws that govern public performances of the work of songwriters and composers. Playing music (even recorded music) inside your business is illegal without paying for the proper licensing. This means that streaming Spotify or Pandora from your personal account, and even bringing in records or CDs from your own collection, could get you into some pretty serious legal trouble and lead to hefty fines. There are a couple of ways to go about treating your clients to brand-supporting tunes without running afoul of the law. You can either obtain a license directly from ASCAP (The American Society of Composers, Authors, and Publishers), who charge you based on how you use music in your salon and then pay songwriters on your behalf for the use of their copyrighted music, or you can work with a business music licensing service that will provide you a selection of music for a flat monthly fee. These service providers will then pay ASCAP on your behalf. There are many affordable business music licensing services to choose from, including SiriusXM satellite radio and Pandora, to name just two. Give some serious thought to how music can enhance your salon's brand, and then choose the service and playlists that are right for you.

Finally, when addressing all of your client's senses, it's important to make sure that your space *smells* nice. Marketers have long known that, just like music, certain scents can influence a customer's behavior. There's even a term for it—*olfactory marketing*. Studies have shown that in-store fragrances can boost impulse purchases, and even alter how people perceive the passage of time. In addition, scientists say that you are a hundred times more likely to remember something that you smell than something that you see, hear, or touch. That's a pretty compelling reason to use fragrance to reinforce your brand identity! In fact, many major retailers and hotel chains now have their own "olfactory logos". This is a growing and complex science, but it's worth considering, even for the small salon owner, how scent can enhance your branding. Keeping in mind your target client and brand story, a special blend of a few essential oils in a diffuser could become your salon's signature scent. Subtlety is critical here though, as many clients can be sensitive to fragrances.

PERFECT PRODUCTS

Something that you'll want to contemplate as you build your salon's brand is the product line (or lines) that you will use and retail in the salon. There are many factors to consider as you make your choices. First, the product line you select for retail should complement your brand and your salon's image. In addition, the price point of the products should align with your market position and appeal to your target client. An exclusive, high-end salon should carry luxury products, for instance, while a salon with a rock-and-roll vibe needs an edgy, youthful retail line. If your spa promotes wellness and natural health and beauty, your customers expect you to use and sell green, plant-based products. Again, don't try to offer something for everyone. It's better to have just one or two relevant product lines that you and your employees know inside and out and are fully invested in, than a cluttered retail area that rivals the drugstore.

And speaking of the drugstore, avoid products from any manufacturer that cannot guarantee salon exclusivity. Whether through diversion or shady back alley corporate deals, we all know that many supposedly "salon only" products end up in big box stores. You can explain the ins and outs of this practice to clients and educate them about why it's important to buy quality products directly from you, but honestly, *why would you want to compete with Walgreens and Target*? Your goal with your branding is to set yourself apart from the competition, and carrying unique retail products that uphold your brand (and that can't be found just anywhere) is one very effective way to do that.

To really ensure that your retail line complements and supports your brand, *private label manufacturing* can be a prudent choice. With this option, you, the salon owner, can work with a private label manufacturing company (a PLM) to choose from a variety of professional product formulas and packaging styles that will be branded and labeled specifically for you. Imagine having your very own shampoos, conditioners, and styling products packaged in your brand colors and named for your salon. Talk about building a brand! While there may be a higher upfront investment in privately labeled products, they will save you money in the long run because you won't be paying a distributor in addition to the manufacturer for them. But, whether you choose traditional distribution routes or create your very own salon products, the retail lines you select for your salon play a meaningful role in your brand's perception and your client's overall experience.

COMMUNICATION IS KEY

One of the most useful qualities a successful hair stylist can possess is the ability to communicate clearly with his or her clients. Anytime a client is in your chair, she should be your sole focus. At no time is this more vital than during a pre-service consultation, especially if she is preparing to make a big change with her cut or color. Before you even drape the client, spend time getting to know her. Ask her about her lifestyle and daily routine, and encourage her to show you photos of the look she hopes to achieve. Be honest with her about what results you can realistically offer and the maintenance involved. Spending a few extra minutes at the beginning of a service ensures that you and your client are on the same page, and can help prevent disappointment and dissatisfaction later.

You have spent countless hours in education and practice, and thousands of dollars to become the beauty expert that you are. More than just an artist, you are an engineer, a chemist, and, often, a therapist. All of these roles are important, but one of the most essential is that of an educator. Clients may leave your chair feeling like a million bucks, but frequently, the first time they shampoo and dry their new hairstyle, they are left frustrated. It's disappointing when they can't recreate the look they left your salon with. Explaining the techniques and products you are using as you style your client's hair empowers them to look their best between salon visits, and reinforces your expertise. Educating clients about the science behind haircolor, chemical services, and the benefits of using professional products strengthens your position as an authority on all things beauty, and can lead to greater trust and higher sales.

When the service ends, many stylists make the mistake of also ending the communication with their client. Don't be one of them. Before she's done processing, ask her if she'd like to pre-book her next appointment, and then walk her to the front desk to be sure that the service is added to your books. Remind her of the products that you used, and ask if she has any questions about how to care for her color or maintain her style at home. To really impress her, place a follow up call a few days after the service asking how she's enjoying her new hairstyle, and if she has any questions. If she is a first time client, you can also over deliver on her expectations by offering her a free blowout that she can redeem in the next few weeks. Establishing that second appointment with her deepens her connection with your brand, and the complementary service makes her feel valued as a client.

And while we're on the subject of communication, there is no surer way to bolster your business and your brand than by collecting a list of your clients' email addresses. You can then use an email marketing service, such as MailChimp or Aweber, to send out branded newsletters letting your clients know about new services, special events, and the latest trends. Not only will you have around the clock access to your clients, regular updates from you will further affix your brand in their minds.

BE A SOCIAL BUTTERFLY

Maintaining a strong social media presence keeps your clients engaged and informed. The number one way to do this is by sharing original, compelling, branded images on Facebook, Twitter, Instagram, and Pinterest. On social media, photos get far more likes, shares, comments, and click-throughs on links than text-based posts do, and this is especially true in a visually rich industry such as ours. Not only do these types of image posts reinforce your brand story, when done well they can lead to shares that will expose new clients to your brand. You can create images highlighting a new service, a seasonal special, or examples of some of your best work—with the client's permission of course. To encourage engagement and shares, your images should appeal directly to your target audience, and match the tone of your branding. Images and graphics that solve problems or inspire your followers are the ones most likely to be shared. Here are some ideas to jumpstart your creativity:

- Create a quick how-to, designed in a grid layout, such as the steps to create an easy holiday party hairstyle, an eye makeup technique, or how to tie a vintage scarf in your hair.

- Highlight the results of using one of the retail products that you carry by creating a dramatic before and after split image.

- Share quick tips or fun facts paired with an engaging image.

- Overlay a great quote about hair or beauty, or one that relates to your salon's branding on a beautiful image or background.

LIFE IS A
CONSTANT
EXCHANGE
—OF—
Beauty
&
WISDOM

Candy's Beauty Bar

Remember that it's important to have the rights to use any image in this way. Just because you found it in Google images doesn't mean that it's free for the taking. There are hundreds of stock photo sites, many of them free, where you can download royalty-free images for use on social media. A list of some of my favorite free stock photo sites can be found in my free Design Resource List at www.thebeautysaloon.net/beautybrandfreegift.

Free online tools like Canva.com and mobile apps, such as Font Studio, make it simple to design eye-catching, shareable social media images for use across all platforms. When creating these, remember the visual brand language you have established for your business. Consistency in font choice, image selection, and color is key. Don't forget to add your website's URL or a subtle watermark with your logo to the image so that new clients can find you if the post goes viral—the best case scenario. It's often easiest to create these kinds of graphics in batches. For consistency and speed, create a single background template that can be used again and again.

Make it easy for your clients to help you gain exposure through clever social media tactics. For instance, you can create a custom Instagram hashtag for clients to use for post-appointment selfies, and hang a nicely framed flyer with instructions on how to do this at your station. Incentivize clients to participate by entering each client who uses your special hashtag in a monthly drawing for a free service or product. This is a mutually beneficial strategy because in addition to the chance to win a prize, clients get to show off their fabulous new looks to their followers, and you get lots of new eyes on your amazing work and beautiful beauty brand.

SHARE THE WEALTH

Keeping your clients content is an investment that will pay off throughout your career. Happy, rewarded clients are more likely to rebook again and again, and are more likely to tell their friends and family about you. Implement a loyalty program offering discounted services after a client visits your salon a certain number of times, or by offering salon gift cards for services or retail based on a simple points-for-dollars-spent system.

Take advantage of branding opportunities here by giving the program a clever name that fits with your brand story. If you can create an air of exclusivity around the program, you'll have even better results, because everyone loves to feel that they are a part of a special club. For The Powder Room, considering my glamorous, vintage brand identity, I might call my rewards program something like *The Lipstick League*, which not only carries implications of a secret girls' society, but also ties in nicely with the powder room primping theme.

When your gratified clients send their friends and family to your chair, deliver the excellent service they've been promised, and then show the referring client your appreciation by offering a free service or product at their next visit, or by granting them additional points in your loyalty program. Creating one big love fest will not only keep your clients delighted, it will also grow your client base exponentially. When you over deliver for every client and show them your appreciation for their business, they will be thrilled to recommend you to everyone they know. Consistently branding each client's individual experience creates an army of devoted brand followers, and that is worth more than any advertisement you can buy.

NOTES

9

Living Your
BRAND

"A brand is a living entity—and it is enriched or undermined cumulatively over time, the product of a thousand small gestures." —Michael Eisner

Whether you own and operate a spacious spa with forty employees, or a boutique salon with a single chair, you are an integral part of your brand. No matter how much thought, effort, and attention to detail you put into telling your brand's story, if you aren't fully and deeply committed to the brand that you're building, your efforts will eventually fall flat. What I'm saying is: You've got to be a ride or die chick when it comes to branding. There's no doing this halfway.

Your brand is the sum of a thousand tiny details, and each impression you create in your clients' minds is the chance to make or break your brand story. Imagine your ideal brand as a brick wall, constantly being built higher, stronger, and better. Every interaction with your clients, no matter how brief, is an opportunity to either add another brick to the wall, or to knock one off. All the beautiful decor and perfect logos in the world won't save you if you aren't living your brand every single day.

When you're building a brand, consistency is the name of the game. We all have off days when we're tired, preoccupied with personal problems, or not feeling our best. Bad days and mistakes are bound to happen, but even when they do, you should strive to deliver excellence to your salon guests, and uphold the brand promise you've made. If you promise a crystal flute of champagne, but deliver a plastic cup of malt liquor, you're going to have a problem. And when those disillusioned clients who were expecting Dom Pérignon take to social media with their Mad Dog 20/20 hangovers, you're going to have a *colossal* problem. A wise philosopher named Yoda once said, "Do or do not. There is no try." I'm pretty sure he was talking about branding.

CULTIVATE YOUR CULTURE

In order to navigate the sometimes choppy waters of the beauty business as a salon owner, you've got to run a tight ship. Employees, if you have them, are as vital to your success as the sailors who keep a battleship afloat. If everyone isn't on the same page, or if your employees aren't treated well and compensated fairly, your business will eventually start to take on water.

It's an unfortunate truth that this industry has a way of attracting folks that thrive on conflict and drama. We've all worked with one—or several—of these stylists over the years, and they can turn even the nicest salon into a toxic environment. As a salon owner, you need a zero tolerance policy for this kind of behavior. A workplace with constant infighting and friction cannot deliver your brand promise to clients. It's just not possible because these kinds of people can't truly care about anyone but themselves, least of all you and your salon's clientele. Their fake smiles and ulterior motives are easily detected by clients and coworkers alike. It's your duty as captain of the ship to hire mature employees that want to grow and succeed, and to treat them with fairness and kindness. As the boss, you set the tone for your salon's environment. Make it one of mutual respect and positivity.

When you cultivate a workplace culture built on integrity and clear communication, you'll be rewarded with loyal, productive employees who want the entire team to succeed, and who champion your brand. More than just a job, a healthy workplace culture fosters deep connections, making employees and coworkers friends and comrades. There are no secrets and whispered conversations, because the lines of communication are open, and employees can be honest with management and with one another.

When employees know that management truly has their interests at heart, they will invest in your vision for your brand along with you. Your clientele will feel the effects of this culture of contentedness when their stylists are happy, relaxed, and free to focus on delivering exceptional service to them. Aim to create a culture in your salon that is so positive, so supportive and wonderful, that when word gets out that you have a job opening, stylists line up around the block to apply.

LOOSE LIPS SINK SHIPS

Sometimes, even the best beauty professionals have trouble setting boundaries. Blame it on the fact that we're part of an industry built around touching the hair, hands, and faces of complete strangers. There's an intimacy to this business not found in any other profession besides medicine. This can be a powerful force for good when you lovingly transform a client, helping her see the beauty that lies within her, or when you lend an ear to her challenges and troubles while she's in your chair, but all that familiarity can make it difficult to draw the line when it comes to what you share in return. If you're a naturally talkative, outgoing person, it can be hard to resist delving too deeply into your personal life when the conversation is flowing. As much as possible, keep it about her, not you.

Of course, you should always strive to be warm and friendly. You don't want to come off as cold or detached, but when interacting with clients, always keep your brand identity at the front of your mind. Idle gossip, foul language, oversharing, or giving clients inside information about the salon's business operations can spell disaster for your brand. You are a skilled beauty professional who has invested time and money in your license and education, not a bartender at a dive bar. Remember that your client has come to you for your brand promise, and whether that promise is luxury, relaxation, or innovative color and cuts, mindless chatter from her stylist shouldn't be on the service menu.

PERSONAL PACKAGING

Would you feel confident ordering a couture evening gown from a fashion designer who arrived at your first fitting in jeans and an old T-shirt? You'd probably expect an in demand designer who commands high fees to wear something more fashionable and refined. Maybe you'd start to doubt whether he was even the right designer for the job. It's no different than you greeting your salon clients with dirty hair in a messy bun while wearing bleach-stained pants. Your clients look up to you as an expert on beauty and the latest trends in hair, makeup, and fashion, and your personal appearance should radiate professionalism and reflect your authority in the industry.

One's attire and appearance are a significant part of their personal brand no matter what their occupation, but as a salon owner or freelance beauty professional, your overall look is doubly important. You can make a favorable impression on clients before you even open your mouth to greet them by creating a purposeful, unique look for yourself. Like Dolly and her tight clothes, lacquered nails, and over-the-top blonde hair, a signature look makes you hard to forget. If you don't already have a strong personal style, take a cue from your North Star List and brand promise when developing your appearance, and let your clothing, hairstyle, makeup, and accessories underline the brand identity you've worked so hard to create.

Many salons opt for an all-black dress code, and it can be a stylish and practical choice. That being said, it may not be the most appropriate look for your salon's branding. Think about the image you want your brand to project, and then design your dress code accordingly. If your brand is all about soft, romantic bridal looks, head-to-toe black could come across as too hard-edged. Your brand would be better served by a more feminine or Bohemian style of dress. Employees of a spa offering primarily esthetic services and facial treatments will enhance their image as skin experts by adopting an all-white, clinical uniform. If you're an authority on bumper bangs and Victory rolls, your wardrobe, hair and makeup should naturally reflect your vintage style. The key is to put some thought into your personal packaging, create a look, and own it.

In our business, good grooming and personal hygiene are even more important than in most. Because we work so closely with our clients—with our armpits literally in their faces at the shampoo bowl—cleanliness and smelling sweet are paramount. Do your best to keep your nails neatly filed and free from stains by wearing gloves any time you're dealing with haircolor, and always keep your eyebrows nicely shaped.

What I'm about to say next might be hard to hear, but I speak the truth: *Your hair and makeup need to be on point every single day.* This is not the business to be in if your look consists primarily of messy ponytails and last night's eyeliner. Sorry, girl. And please resist the temptation to work on clients while your own head is covered in foils. Save your personal cuts and color for when you're off the clock. I know time for taking care of yourself is tight, but there's no quicker way to show clients how unprofessional you are than to turn your salon environment into something resembling a junior high slumber party.

BRING THEM CLOSER

You will never have a brand as big and iconic as Coca-Cola or Nike, and that's okay. Success on a global scale brings its own set of problems. When companies grow to a massive size, the focus often moves away from brand awareness, which they have plenty of. Instead, the challenge becomes how to humanize the brand and create an emotional connection with the customer.

Another sage philosopher, the one-of-a-kind Snoop D-O-Double G, once said, "A lot of brands, you can't touch them. When you're dealing with Snoop Dogg, he brings you closer to the brand and it feels like it's a part of you." Clients can't touch Starbucks or

Apple, but, like Snoop, if you conduct yourself in a way that speaks directly to them and makes your brand promise real, they'll be invested in your story. Huge corporations struggle with keeping their thousands of employees and millions of consumer impressions "on brand". As a small business owner, you have the advantage when it comes to customer connection, because you *are* your brand. Your greatest asset in branding is *you*. Living authentically and conducting business with integrity will do more for your branding efforts than any slick website or social media campaign.

But living your brand requires loving your brand, so build something original and credible that you can be proud of, and then go all in. Be an ambassador for your brand, not just inside your salon, but everywhere you go. Carry yourself with dignity and confidence, treat clients and coworkers with fairness and kindness, and always be true to your vision and values. There is no magic bullet—building a brand takes time, hard work, and dedication, but the results are invaluable.

WHAT WILL YOU BUILD?

So, now you've learned exactly what branding is and why it's so crucial to your success. You've chosen your niche, identified your ideal client, defined your position in the market, and created a North Star List to guide you through all your branding decisions. You know what makes a salon name great, how to go about designing a professional-looking logo, and how creating a strong visual brand language across all print and social media outlets will reinforce your brand awareness. You understand the role color plays in your branding efforts, and how your salon's decor can reinforce your brand's story. Finally, you now know methods for branding every detail of your client's experience, and just how crucial it is to live your brand on a daily basis.

What will you do with this information? What will you create? How will you begin working toward your goals today? Whether you own an established salon, are in the planning stages of freelancing or booth rental, or even if you're just stepping out of those cosmetology school doors into the big, dazzling world of the beauty industry, you now have the power to design and grow your salon business far beyond your wildest imagination. You are the architect of your future. The concepts and skills you've learned in this book will serve as your blueprint as you build the beautiful salon business of your dreams.

NOTES

Holly Hall is an artist, writer, and licensed cosmetologist. She has worked in the beauty industry for over a decade, and is passionate about helping other beauty professionals grow their businesses and achieve their dreams. She lives in Oklahoma with her musician husband and three children where she studies history and makes creative messes.

In addition to creating vintage-inspired art, gifts, and business cards for salon professionals, Holly writes about the beauty business from a vintage viewpoint at TheBeautySaloon.net.

BUILD YOUR BEAUTY BRAND
Quick Start Branding Action Plan

THIS BONUS WORKBOOK INCLUDES:

BUILD YOUR BEAUTY BRAND

FIND Your Niche, **CAPTIVATE** Your Clients, And **GROW** The Salon Business Of Your **DREAMS**

HOLLY I. HALL

- Branding Steps Checklist
- Find Your Niche Worksheet
- Target Client Worksheet
- North Star List Worksheet
- Salon Naming Worksheet
- Visual Brand Language Style Guide
- Design Resource Link List that includes:

  Graphic Design Tools
  Color Tools
  Free Stock Photo Sites
  D.I.Y. Salon Design Ideas

TheBeautySaloon.net

As a thank you for buying this book, and to help you take immediate action to begin building the brand of your dreams, I want to give you a FREE bonus workbook which includes a Branding Steps Checklist and much more to get you started the right way.

Download the free workbook at:

thebeautysaloon.net/beautybrandfreegift

Made in the USA
Middletown, DE
28 July 2017